Jiu-Jitsu

*The Ultimate Quick Start
Guide To Dominate
Jiu-Jitsu*

George Silva

Disclaimer Notice:

Please note the information contained within this document is for educational and entertainment purposes only. Every attempt has been made to provide accurate, up to date and reliable complete information. No warranties of any kind are expressed or implied. Readers acknowledge that the author is not engaging in the rendering of legal, financial, medical or professional advice.

By reading this document, the reader agrees that under no circumstances are we responsible for any losses, direct or indirect, which are incurred as a result of the use of information contained within this document, including, but not limited to, —errors, omissions, or inaccuracies.

Table of Contents

Page

Introduction

I want to thank you and congratulate you for downloading the book, *"Jiu-Jitsu: The Ultimate Quick Start Guide To Dominate Jiu-Jitsu"*.

This book will teach you everything you need to know about this ancient Japanese martial art, from its origins and philosophy to hands-on techniques and exercises to help you along your journey to mastering Jiu-Jitsu.

Important aspects of the mind frame necessary to succeed are discussed as well. Like so many other martial arts, the strongest opponent one might face during their Jiu-Jitsu training is themselves. Maintaining positive attitude and avoiding frustration are absolutely essential.

The pages that follow aim to give you a well-rounded picture of what it takes to succeed in your training as well as the guidelines for the training itself.

Thanks again for downloading this book, I hope you enjoy it!

Chapter 1

Jiu-Jitsu Origins And Philosophy

Jiu-Jitsu is a martial art created during the Sengoku period of Japanese history (15th and 16th century). It represents a combination of several martial arts, combined into one to be used in close combat. In situations where usage of weapons was not possible, warriors had to resort to their arms and legs to subdue the enemy.

The name itself is a compound made of two Japanese words: *jiu* (or ju) meaning soft, flexible or gentle and *jitsu* (jutsu), which translates as a technique or art. As one can guess from this compound, Jiu-Jitsu is primarily a defensive form.

The underlying philosophy of this martial art is using your opponent's strength against him as opposed to trying to subdue him with your own strength. In close combat situations, in particular against fully armored enemies, using brute force and forceful strikes proved rather ineffective.

As a solution, Japanese came up with a fighting form that was based primarily on ways to quickly incapacitate one's opponent and neutralize the threat.

Moves involving choking, throwing, and joint locks proved to be very useful for these purposes.

In addition, the oldest form of Jiu-Jitsu, called *Takenouchi-ryu*, also taught the art of combat using short weapons, like daggers and short sticks. When an enemy was near, long weapons, no matter how powerful otherwise, were quite useless. Short ones, on the other hand, were easy to wield and use to both, attack and block the attacks of the enemy.

Overall, jiu jitsu is the most ancient martial art, perfect, complete and efficient self-defense. Its origin despite contradictory is attributed to China after India, Japan and Brazil, where it developed, improved and became the world center of this precious art. The sports jiu jitsu is the competitive part where athletes display their technical, physical and psychological skills in order to achieve victory over your opponents. Valid blows are those who seek to neutralize, immobilize, choke, push, twist joints, as well as throw your opponent to the ground by falls, while non-valid blows, considered unfair, such as biting, hair pulling, sticking fingers in the eyes, reach the genitals, sprain fingers or any other process to traumatize with the use of hands, elbows, head, knees and feet.

Jiu-Jitsu continues to develop during the 17th century. Influenced by the philosophy of Neo-Confucianism, the Tokugawa shogunate strived to decrease all war activities. This meant that weapons and armor became a thing of the past while hand-to-hand combat skills started to flourish.

What this meant for Jiu-Jitsu, in particular, was that some changes needed to be introduced. Since the opponents were now mostly unarmored, certain new strikes were introduced as well. Earlier striking techniques were usually focused on exposed areas of the head, like eyes and throat. These new techniques were tested for a while, but in the end, it was concluded that they were not effective enough and that they used too much energy. By the end of 18th century, striking in Jiu-Jitsu became limited to purposes of distracting opponents and throwing them off balance before implementing a much more efficient lock or a throw.

The martial art that is predominantly encountered today is, in fact, *Edo* Jiu-Jitsu, which developed during the Edo period (1603 - 1868). These combat systems were designed for fighting unarmed opponents and not for use on a battlefield. Many core techniques involve *atemi waza*, which understands striking your opponent in different vital organs, which obviously would not work against armored enemies.

Although it is not commonly found in Jiu-Jitsu today, the application of different weapons, like daggers, iron fans, and *hojo* cords to subdue the opponent was often the essential part of the training in the past. However, the Tokyo police even today carry hojo cords, which can be used to restrain or strangle an attacker if necessary.

Modern forms of Jiu-Jitsu are often referred to as Gendai. These variations have mostly come to life after the period of Meiji Restoration (1866 - 1869). Most of Gendai Jiu-Jitsu schools do not have direct links to the traditional systems, as there is little need to train the skills one would use against an armored opponent in the modern age.

Gendai Jiu-Jitsu is widely applied by the police and military forces around the world and especially in Japan. Because its primary goal is to incapacitate and subdue the adversary, often without inflicting any serious damage, it is a perfect fit for the type of work the police performs on a daily basis.

Chapter 2

Modern Derivatives Of Jiu-Jitsu

Jiu-Jitsu has had an influence on the development of a number of martial arts, which went on to develop as separate skills in their own right. While many elements have been significantly changed or completely removed, Jiu-Jitsu still served as the starting point and the foundation for these martial arts.

Judo

Judo is perhaps the most famous martial art that has its origins in Jiu-Jitsu. It was developed in Japan in 1882, by Kano Jigoro. The meaning of the word literally translates as "gentle way," so even the name of the discipline is quite similar to Jiu-Jitsu.

Like the former, judo is based on techniques to subdue your opponents through various moves which involve throwing, choking and joint locks. Strikes and pushes are a part of judo training but are not allowed at sports competitions.

Kano took principles of Jiu-Jitsu, but he wanted to develop them further and, in doing so, raise the judo from a martial art to a martial way. This meant removing the elements that were not in line with the Confucian philosophy and creating a discipline that does not serve only its own purpose, but would also lead to the betterment of the society in general.

While it quickly became quite popular in Japan, it wasn't until the 1956 World Judo Championships that the sport received wider recognition. Kano Jigoro, the founder, was not particularly interested in seeing judo become an Olympic sport, but he was not opposed to the idea either. His only fear was that the art could be tainted by nationalism and competition, which he saw as a step backward.

Regardless, judo was introduced to the 1964 Olympic Games in Tokyo as a discipline for men. The first women's event took place in 1988 and in 1992 it became an official part of the Olympics.

Brazilian Jiu-Jitsu

Another derivative of the original martial art, Brazilian Jiu-Jitsu is a defense technique, martial art, and a sports discipline. It developed indirectly, as a branch of judo, and eventually became distinct enough to warrant a separate name altogether.

One of the main focus points of Brazilian Jiu-Jitsu is the ground combat. It is based on the conviction that even a smaller, physically weaker opponent can defeat a stronger one if they use the techniques correctly and if they can bring the battle to the ground, where the conditions are not as unfavorable for the smaller person.

The first Jiu-Jitsu / judo school opened in Brazil in 1909. With the arrival of Mitsuyo Maeda, one of Kano's emissaries sent out to the world to explain the "jiu-do" (judo) philosophy, in 1914, the discipline took a somewhat different direction. Maeda took on brothers Gracie as his students and they, in turn, created a different judo variation that came to be known as Brazilian Jiu-Jitsu.

In 1917, a teenager named Carlos Gracie (1902-1994) saw the first time in Bethlehem, a presentation of the Japanese who was able to overpower and finish the giants of the region. A friend of his father, Gastao Gracie, Maeda agreed to teach for the fidgety boy the art of defending. In his classes, he taught Carlos and other Brazilians - as Luiz France, later to be master of Oswaldo Fadda - the concepts of his art: standing or on the ground, the opponent's strength should be the weapon for victory; to approach the opponent, the use of low kicks and elbows should be the artifices before taking him to the ground.

Faithful student, Carlos Gracie embraces the Jiu-Jitsu and, for mother's regret that dreamed see more diplomats in the famous family, began to instill in brothers the love for art. One among eight brothers (Oswaldo, Gastao Jr., George, Helena, Helio, Mary and Ilka), Carlos opened in 1925, the Gracie family's first Jiu-Jitsu academy. In the newspapers, the ad was a masterpiece of marketing: "If you want to have a broken arm come to the Gracie academy."

Lately, Brazilian Jiu-Jitsu (BJJ) has been gaining a lot of popularity, and there are numerous school across the globe teaching it.

Sports Jiu-Jitsu

In order to be considered a sport, Jiu-Jitsu had to undergo some very crucial transformations. Many of the concepts found in traditional teachings are not very sporty, which is hardly surprising if we consider the original intention of this martial art.

Today, three main types of sports Jiu-Jitsu can be seen at various competitions.

Duo is a self-defense demonstration. The defender (uke) and the attacker (tori) are from the same team, and they present different self-defense techniques. Although they belong to the same team, they do not know what attack comes next, as that is determined by the judges.

Fighting system (or free fighting) is exactly what it sounds like. Two opponents try to subdue one another using various Jiu-Jitsu techniques, but there is a strong emphasis on safety and fairness.

The Brazilian (or grappling) system involves two standing up opponents who try to bring one another to the ground. In this particular variation, no striking is allowed whatsoever.

Chapter 3

Jiu Jitsu Benefits

• Decreases stress

• Self-defense for both men and women

• Uninhibits shy and calms the agitated and anxious

• Increase self-esteem, self-confidence and develops character (individual achievement in sport)

• Works and sets the body like the arms, abdomen and hip, both men and women

• Increases the body's resistance

• Accelerates metabolism

• Improves cardiovascular and respiratory capacity

• Increases flexibility

• Increases coordination

• Increases the reflexes

Who Should Practice Jiu Jitsu

• It is suitable for those looking for a sport that works both physical and mental, often says that jiu-jitsu turns little boys into good men and of good character.

• It is indicated for people who aim to increase cardiovascular capacity and avoid future risk of heart or breathing problems, since it requires a lot of physical condition of the practitioner, however, you'll reach advanced levels of fitness in steps, anyone can achieve advanced levels of fitness it's enough the physical determination.

• Children should practice the sport, the minimum age varies from 5 to 8 years. Help on growth and body development, mental (disciplinary) and it is also recreational becoming a fun and distancing young people from drugs, cigarettes and drinks, given that fighters are always disciplined with food and rest.

What Is The Jiu Jitsu Caloric Expenditure

• 750 Kcal / H,usually burns a practitioner with some certain experience that can complete all of the jiu jitsu warm up, and may increase the caloric burn through aerobic and anaerobic exercises. In more advanced jiu-jitsu class can lose up to 1,500 Kcal / class.

Minimun Period To Feel The Difference In The Body

• The practitioner begins to feel difference in the body and the conditions of fight between 4 to 6 months of practice of sport, with a minimum frequency of three times a week. This period may be reduced if associated to good nutrition, minimum period of body recovery (muscles) and mainly determination of the practitioner.

• In terms of fighting efficiency and individual skill, frequency and attention can make miracles, usually within 3 months of jiu-jitsu a white belt already has the capacity to fight other fighters at any level. This is achieved by the objectives pursued during the fight which varies according to the degree, those are the resources to achieve these goals.

Note: The interesting jiu-jitsu is that how the fight becomes unpredictable, you never know how a fight will end when two opponents are confronting, it is the true body of chess so it is practiced by famous and intelligent people. Jiu-jitsu is not violence or cowardice, is especially efficiency, equilibrium and peace of mind.

What To Eat Before Jiu Jitsu Training?

The feed before training is very important to ensure the necessary energy for physical activity. The player can eat a small meal 1h before training, or a large meal (avoiding excess fat and fiber, which delay digestion) up to 3 hours earlier.

What To Eat After Jiu Jitsu Training?

At this stage it becomes necessary intake of foods rich in carbohydrates to replenish the muscle wasting, facilitating recovery of the individual. This meal should be made after 2 hours (maximum) of the end of the training, as this is the period when the stimulus for energy replacement is sharp.

What happens when someone starts practicing Jiu-Jitsu?

An ordinary person suddenly decides to practice a martial art, going to a gym and is faced with numerous possibilities. Boxing, Judo, Karate, Aikido, Kung Fu, Muay Thay, among others, but for being a fan of fights, and from an early age like to see events like Pride, UFC etc .. at that time was called the "anything goes". This person decides to practice Jiu-Jitsu!

Often without quite knowing what it is Jiu-Jitsu, just having the awareness that the "heroes" of those events that attended (Rickson, Royce, Minotauro), were specialists in the art, this person decides to buy the kimono and start attend classes. And those first classes are just a "setting" serve only to give a "north" for the beginner, basic positions, posture, movement, are things that students learn, and as a basis for any further teaching. The student often innocent and not having the slightest idea of what is the gentle art, in turn, after learning how to apply an "Americana from mount," has the feeling that may compete on equal terms with a heavyweights fighter champion.

It is then at this point, that after 3 or 4 classes, the instructor, invites you to train, ie "take a roll". The pupil in turn, all excited to put into action "all" those techniques he learned, is placed promptly in combat position. The instructor, takes a look to the other corner of the room, for that small and weak student, who must weigh about 15 kilograms less, but in his belt, but still white, are set 4 degrees. The puny pupil starts walking toward the training position while the first pupikl, not realizing that the small and puny teammate is on the verge of trading belt, talk to yourself:

- The instructor must be crazy! I will destroy this runt!

An honest mistake, the forward roll starts, and 15 seconds the thin take his companion's arm, thinking the student is something like:

- Pure Luck! I will not drag one's feet, now it's for real!

It is then that he fell upon with all his force, and the thin boy, trying to control the breath and calmly, sweeps, mounts and finish by applying a cross choke.

And so, it took 5 minutes of training, in which the puny boy although arrived tired at the end of the rolls, finished the teammate over 10 times in a row.

Meanwhile, the beginner student, unable to breathe properly, has the impression that we were the longer 5 minutes of your life and still incredulous at what happened, begin to have some idea of how far you can get in the gentle art .

In this way, it is that other training sessions are held, always training with different people, each with more experience, others with less, and that is how the student begins to like Jiu-Jitsu, what was supposed to be a hobby, it becomes an addiction!

Helio Gracie, one of the great patriarchs of Jiu-Jitsu, said that Jiu-Jitsu is designed to help mainly small and puny people!

Chapter 4

Jiu-Jitsu Techniques

Now that you have acquainted yourself with the history, background, and the philosophy of the martial art, it is time to learn about some of the most essential techniques of Jiu-Jitsu.

We have already seen that the basic premise of Jiu-Jitsu and all its derivatives is using your opponent's strength and size to your advantage. These techniques aim to achieve that very effect. Often, being at a physical disadvantage does not necessarily mean an inevitable defeat.

Kicks and punches

As we have explained, kicks and punches are not the essential part of Jiu-Jitsu, but there are still a few moves that you should be aware of to give yourself the best odds in combat.

1) *Front snap punch* is executed from a close distance and from a fighting stance. First out is the left fist, which only slightly touches your opponent and prepares for the real strike. Right fist follows next, as the left comes back. Add some extra power to the attack by twisting your hips.

2) *Front snap kick* aims to strike the attacker in the groin. It starts from the fighting stance, with lifting up your rear leg knee up to the height of your hips. Then, launch the strike by snapping the foot out and go back to your initial position.

3) *Reverse twist punch* is used when the attacker tries to land a punch. Block his attack by the left forearm and lower your right hand to the height of your hips. From that position, strike the attacker in the plexus with your right hand. You can add extra force to your strike by bending the front knee.

4) *Snap kick* (with one front step) is delivered from the fighting stance. It is performed similarly to the front snap kick, but the difference is in the ending phase. After striking, you will place the right foot in front of your left one, closing down the gap between you and the attacker.

5) *Elbow strike* is best applied when in close proximity of the attacker. Hit the opponent with your elbow right under the chin, while keeping your right hand as close as possible to your right shoulder. To gain extra momentum, try to twist on the right foot while delivering the blow.

6) *Back fist - reverse twist combo.* First, strike with your back fist and hit the side of your attacker's head. Have the right hand prepared at the hip height and, as you retract the left hand, strike with the other one and punch the attacker in plexus.

7) *Roundhouse kick* can be very powerful as it delivers a blow to the attackers leg, upper body or head. It can be a bit tricky to perform as you need to spin anti-clockwise on your left foot, bringing the right knee to the hip level. Next, snap out your foot and strike.

8) *Ridge hand strike*, if done correctly, can be very powerful. Tuck your thumb into the palm, creating the ridge-hand with the boney part of your hand. Deliver the strike to the sensitive areas like neck, nose or the jaw. However, it can lead to the injuries of your hand or the arm if not done correctly.

9) *Crescent kick* is primarily used to break the attacker's guard. As you are facing your opponents standing in the combat position, recline on the back foot and swing the front leg, drawing an imaginary circle with your foot. This should break your attacker's guard and get you in the position to start lending serious punches.

10) *Two-point combo*. The strike combines two kicks into a single attack: a front snap kick and a side snap kick. You begin with bringing your right knee to the hip height and striking out with a front snap kick. After you hit your attacker's groin, bring the foot back, maintaining the knee leveled with your hips. Turn anti-clockwise on your left foot and attack again with your right foot. You can once again aim for the attacker's groin or to his knee.

11) *Three-point combo*. This move combines three different kicks: front snap kick, back fist, and a

roundhouse kick. It begins with a front snap kick. After you strike, bring the right foot in front of your left foot. Your opponent will likely move back to try and avoid your next attack. At this point, you strike with a roundhouse kick to the leg or body. Finally, finish the combination off with the back fist to your attacker's head.

Blocks and parries

Blocks and parries are ways to prevent your attacker from delivering kicks and punches and thus stopping them from possibly incapacitating you and ending the combat.

1) *Inside forearm block.* When your attacker tries to punch, lift up the left forearm and use it to block his hand. At the same time, lower the right hand to your hip and move forward with your left foot to close down the distance.

2) *Leg block* is applied against a roundhouse kick. As your attacker moves to strike, rotate on your right foot and push your right arm behind in order to meet and block the kick.

3) *Head block* is used against an attacker trying to strike the top of your head, using his hand or an object. Use the left forearm to block the incoming attack, while, once again, lowering the right hand to your hip and putting the left foot out to close the gap.

4) *Low parry* can help you prevent the snap kick. You should use the same side the attacker is using to strike

to block the kick (if they attack with right leg, use the right hand, and vice versa). As your attacker tries to deliver the strike, use your hand to grab his ankle and prevent him from completing the move.

5) High parry will serve you best against straight or hook punches. Once again, use the same hand to block the punch as your attacker. You use one hand to deflect the attack while the other one remains at the hip level.

Locks

Locks are defensive strategies, but unlike blocks, they are used to move from the position of the defender to the position of the attacker. Once you have successfully performed a lock, you will be the one with the upper hand and, often, with a decisive advantage.

1) *Straight arm lock.* When your attacker tries to deliver an uppercut to your stomach region, block them using the left hand downward block. After that, grab their wrist and rotate clockwise on your left foot and move to the side of your attacker. From this position, deliver an elbow strike to your attacker's head. Next, wrap your left hand around the attacker's arm and twist their wrist towards the floor to lock them down.

2) *A shoulder lock* is the best defense against an uppercut punch. When your attacker moves in to deliver the punch, step forward on your left foot. Use the left hand downward block to stop his punch.

Strike the attacker with the open palm of your right hand in the shoulder. Next, pull his shoulder down and move your left hand under their right hand. Move to the side of the attacker and place the left hand on top of your right hand, so that the attackers hand is now reclining on your left shoulder. You can finish the move by delivering a knee strike.

3) *Elbow lock* is another technique used against the uppercut punch. As your attacker tries to deliver the punch, move forward and block their attempt with the left hand downward block. With your right hand, grab the attackers elbow from the backside and pull it to the side, while still maintaining contact with your left hand as well. Wrap the left hand around the attackers elbow and place it on their back, freeing the right hand. You can finish the move with a right knee kick.

4) *Back hammer lock* is performed identically to the elbow lock up to the point where you place your left hand on the opponent's back. Now, use your free right hand to grab their wrist. Take the left hand off the attacker's elbow and grab your own wrist. Your opponent's movements are now very limited, and he is in a perfect position to receive a finishing knee kick to the head.

5) *Wrist locks* are a great way to defend and start a counterattack when your attacker tries to push you or grab your shirt (or lapel). They require very little force and energy but still, they are very efficient. Wrist locks can be used to bring your opponent straight to the ground or position them to deliver a punch or kick.

Twisting your attacker's wrist will make it very hard for them to defend.

Escapes

While locks are very efficient in incapacitating your opponent, knowing how to escape the locks is equally important, especially when facing a skilled attacker. These are some of the basic escapes that can come in very hand during combat.

1) *Escaping wrist grab*. As we have seen, the wrist grab is one of the most used locks, because it does not require a lot of energy to implement. In order to escape it, move your hand to the left, bringing it in front of your face in such a fashion that you are facing the palm. Rotate the hand clockwise and thrust it down to the right to set yourself free from the grip.

2) *Escaping front strangle*. When you are facing an attacker, who is trying to strangle you, move your right foot to the back to slightly loosen the strange, and place your right hand in front of your face to protect from a potential head strike. Lift the left hand up in the air and use it to punch forcefully through the attackers arms and remove the grip. Once free, move the left hand back up and elbow-punch the opponent in the face.

3) *Escaping back strangle*. If an attacker tries to strangle you from the back, move your left foot, so you get position on the side of the aggressor. Then, strike with the right elbow, aiming for the attacker's

stomach. Place the right hand on his back and grab his right bicep with the left hand. Move the right foot in front of the attacker's right foot, while stretching the left leg further to the left and bending it in the knee. Finally, spin the upper body anti-clockwise, causing the opponent to fall to the ground.

4) *Escaping bear hug.* If your attacker tries to use the bear hug from the back, with your hands inside, you can utilize the following technique to break free. Make a small jump and stretch your legs to the sides, to lower your body. While doing this, thrust up with your arms to break free from the grip. Once your hands are free, grab the attacker's right hand over your shoulder and do a stepping shoulder throw.

5) *Escaping head locks.* There are several different ways to escape head locks, depending on what seems like the best solution in any given situation.

a) If the attacker has you in the side head lock, move your left arm around his back and grab his left arm, to prevent him from punching you. With your right hand, grab the wrist of his right hand. Stand up forcefully, pulling the attacker's arm to the side.

b) If you find yourself in the side headlock, you can also break the lock by grabbing your attacker's left shoulder and bracing their left foot to prevent them from moving backward. Finally, sit down to throw the opponent to the ground and take the mounted position to gain the advantage.

c) Another way to escape the side headlock is using the stomach throw. While locked, grab the attacker's collar with your left hand. Use the right hand to punch his stomach, grabbing the belt. Twist anti-clockwise and lay to the ground, throwing the attacker over your head. Try to perform these moves as fast as possible to maintain the momentum and gather the energy necessary for the throw.

Throws

Different throws and throw-kick combos are the essential moves of Jiu-Jitsu. These are the techniques that best reflect the philosophy of this martial art of using your attacker's strength against him, instead of trying to overpower them using your own power and energy.

1) *Body drop.* Your attacker tries to punch you. You block the punch with the basic forearm block and move your left foot towards the opponent's left foot. Spin anti-clockwise on the left foot, grabbing the attacker's back with your right hand while gripping the bicep of their left hand. Move the right foot in front of the attacker's right foot, while stretching the left leg further to the left and bending it in the knee. Spin the upper body anti-clockwise, sweeping the attacker's right leg, forcing him to the ground. Once on the ground, move the left hand round the attacker's right arm, behind the elbow, completing the arm lock.

2) *Recumbent ankle throw.* This throw begins with your attacker attempting a strike that you can block

using the head block. While blocking, step forward with the left foot and place the right foot behind the attacker's right ankle. Do a right side breakfall, keeping the right foot in the same position and then move the left foot just under the opponent's right knee. Pull the right foot and push with the left one to bring the attacker down on his back. When he falls down, rise on both hands and deliver the stamp kick to the attacker's groin region.

3) *Hip throw with a strike*. This is the technique best used against the straight punch. Block the punch with the forearm block, moving the left foot forward. Twist anti-clockwise on the right foot, pulling the right arm behind the opponent's back. Pull the feet back together. Bend the knees, leaning forward and pulling the attacker onto your back. Once the opponent is reclining on your back, straighten the legs, lifting him from the ground and throw him off your back. The best finishing move is a simple straight punch.

4) *Half shoulder throw* begins with the simple inside forearm block of the attacker's punch. As you block, move the right foot forwards and place yourself sideways to the opponent. Deliver the elbow punch to the attacker's ribs and then move the right arm up, grabbing him under his right armpit with the inside of your arm. Bend the knees, pulling the attacker onto your back, then straighten them up again to lift him off the ground. At this point, just throw the opponent off your back with a simple body twist, finishing up with a punch or an arm lock.

5) *Wrist lock - throw combo.* Once again, the technique used against the straight punch. When the attacker moves in to deliver the strike, rotate clockwise on the left foot and grab the attacker's wrist with your left hand. Next, grab the wrist with your right hand as well to tighten the grip. Spin on the left foot to get in a position parallel and slightly behind the attacker on his right side, with your back facing his back. Keep twisting, while moving down to your left knee to get the attacker out of the balance and to the ground. Once on the ground, place the right knee on the attacker's right arm and push his palm to the floor.

6) *Drawing ankle throw* needs to be performed fast, in order to fully utilize your attacker's momentum against them. As they move in to deliver a straight punch, use the basic inside forearm block and move the right foot to the right, so to place yourself facing the side of the attacker's head. Your left foot should be placed next to the attacker's leading foot, bracing his ankle. Next, move the right hand under the attacker's left armpit and then just push it to the left. Because of your left foot positioning, the attacker will be thrown to the ground.

7) *Knee wheel throw* is useful against the straight punch. Once again, block the strike with the inside forearm block and move the left foot forward and to the left. Apply the ridge hand strike to the attacker's main artery in the neck. If powerful enough, it can cause the opponent to nearly lose his conscience. Once

you have done this, push the attacker's left shoulder to disturb his balance and place the right foot right behind his right knee. Thrust forward with your right hand, while pushing with the right foot and sweep the attacker to the ground.

8) *Stamp throw.* If the attacker tries to strike with the straight punch, move the left foot forward and block with the inside forearm. Spin anti-clockwise on the left foot, moving the right arm behind the opponent's back. Bend the left knee to pull the attacker onto your back, while lifting your right leg, getting ready for the stamp. Stamp the right foot on the right side of the floor while twisting the upper body and finish the throw.

9) *Rice bale throw* is used against an uppercut punch. As your attacker tries to strike, block him using the downward block with your left hand and respond with the right-handed uppercut to the attacker's stomach. As they bend, wrap your right arm around the opponent's neck and firmly grab your right wrist with your left hand. Next, cover the attacker's right foot with your right foot, sit back and roll the opponent over your head. Turn around and get up on your knees, firmly holding the attacker in a guillotine choke.

10) *Sweeping loin throw.* This is a technique to be used when the attacker strikes with a straight punch. Move your left foot forward and use the forearm block to stop the attack. Next, rotate anti-clockwise on the left foot, pulling your right arm behind the attacker's

back. Bend the left knee, so you can pull the opponent onto your back. Lift up your right foot, preparing to perform the sweep. To finish the throw, straighten the left leg, lifting the attacker off the ground and sweep his legs with your right foot. Twist the upper body and throw your opponent to the ground.

11) *Front scissors throw* comes in play when the attacker tries to strike with an uppercut to the stomach. Move forward and to the left with the left foot, positioning yourself so to deflect the punch using your right hand. Next, step forward with the right foot to move behind the attacker's right foot.

Now, extend your left foot in front the attacker and raise the right leg so to position it behind his knees, ready to swipe him down. Finally, scissor the legs to throw the attacker off the balance and get him to the ground. You should be in favorable position to gain the upper hand over your attacker and finish him off.

Breakfalls

Breakfalls are unique techniques in Jiu-Jitsu used to minimize the damage caused by a fall, which often follows after a throw. Having good breakfall skills is equally important as knowing how to land punches or make locks. They are often a crucial part of different throws as well, so make sure to at least get the basic techniques right.

1) *Side breakfall.* Standing with your feet level, move the right foot to the front and left of the right foot.

Then, let yourself fall to the right side, throwing the right arm on the floor as you touch the ground. This will break the fall, making the landing much softer, without causing any significant damage. When you land, position yourself in a protective stance, with your knee lifted to protect the groin area and hands up to cover the head.

2) *Back breakfall.* From standing, move to a crouching position, with arms crossed on your chest and your chin tucked down. Next, allow yourself to fall on your back, spreading your arms to the sides while landing. You can also thrust your legs forward from the ground to prepare to push away an attacker in front of you.

3) *Front breakfall.* Start with standing, your feet level. Slightly bend your knees and jump while thrusting your legs out behind you. Simultaneously, start lifting the hands to the height of your face. When landing, break the fall using your forearms and make sure to turn the head sideways, to make sure your nose does not get injured.

4) *Backward rolling breakfall.* This breakfall is used when someone pushes you. As you fall to the ground, tuck your chin into the chest and land on the back, with your arms spread to the sides to soften the landing. Next, roll over one shoulder and return to the fighting stance, facing your opponent.

5) *Spinning side breakfall.* Standing with the left foot forward, imagine you are holding someone's belt on

the left side and make a leap over your right shoulder. As you fall, you should land on your left side, slamming the arm on the ground to make the landing softer.

Chapter 5

Defensive and Submissions - step by step

The Triangle

The Triangle is an original position of Judo, adapted (very good by the way) to Jiu Jitsu. This is a choke, where that who applying, use both legs to wrap around the neck and one of the opponent's arms, reducing the space and running to finish.

How to run the triangle

When the opponent attempts to fit the triangle, you must be in position immediately, preventing he can pull your head.

Soon after, one must cross the hand that is outside the triangle, and get the opposite collar of his opponent, causing pressure. After that, you must run the guard pass by pushing with the arm and the shoulder.

Jiu-Jitsu - Triangle Escape

Tip for the defense of the Triangle.

The main tip for those who want to defend the triangle is to stay calm and do the posture. If you can do the posture correctly, certainly you'll be able to defend the triangle and several other Jiu Jitsu positions.

Leg Lock from Closed Guard

What is Leg Lock in the Jiu Jitsu?

The Leg Lock ends the opponent exerting counter pressure to the knee joint, causing the opponent to give up the fight. It is important to emphasize that this is a very fair position and requires expertise to the application because if applied incorrectly can seriously hurt your teammate. This position is prohibited to Purple, Blue and White belts, being released only Brown and Black belts.

The Leg Lock from Closed Guard, is a relatively simple position of Jiu Jitsu, ideal for those who recently took the brown belt, and want to increase the positions of the closed guard, without attacking arms or neck.

Detail of Position

A very important detail is that we can highlight the position of the hip compared to the opponent's knee. Your hips should be positioned just above the opponent's knee, so as to form a leverage point and that you use the minimum force, obtaining maximum efficiency in completion.

The Bow and Arrow Choke

This choke if applied at the right time, it is very difficult to defend, and their success rate in submission is very large, it is worth training this position and have it in your arsenal.

Details Bow and Arrow Choke

When you are in the back of your opponent, your drive must be to apply the traditional choke back, opening the lapel.

At this time, your opponent will position the body towards the ground in order to defend the choke, in this time, you will put the arm on the ground to prevent it can defend. After that, you will do one of the hooks, and your leg on the other side, you put in the hip, grabbing his opponent. After mastery over the opponent, you will cross the leg that was on the abdomen of the opponent, and with the arm that is on the ground, you will seek and hold the trousers of the opponent.

Ending in the bow and arrow position

In the final movement of the bow and arrow choke, you will close the elbow that is holding the collar, put his leg over the shoulder of the opponent, and make the move like closing the guard. After that just continue with the pressure and finish the fight.

Arm Bar from Closed Guard

It is one of the basic positions of Jiu Jitsu, one of the first positions that you learn when you start Jiu Jitsu training, the famous arm bar from closed guard.

Ending with the arm bar

Despite being a basic and easy to perform, is extremely efficient, especially in its power to end because you use all the strength of her legs and her hips against the opponent's elbow.

Details of Position

The arm bar from closed guard has some variations depending on your body type, and also depending on the way the opponent is doing the posture. But the mechanics of motion, is basically the same and consists of 3 steps:

Break posture

You should make your opponent will be with the "broken" posture without dominant grip, hindering its defense power.

Domain arm to being attacked

Since the beginning of the movements, you should keep in mind that the arm will be attacked, and especially you should have dominion over this arm.

Hip Escape

The hip escape is present in virtually all of Jiu Jitsu positions, and the arm bar from closed guard is no different. You must move your hips fairly toward the arm that will be attacked.

Running these 3 three steps consistently, you will have great chances of getting finish your opponent.

6 principles to improve your Open Guard in Jiu Jitsu

Make guard is an art! It requires flexibility, patience, strength and technique, a lot of technique.

The six principles are:

1- Opening of Guard

Keep in mind: If you opened your guard for free will, you are throwing open guard. But now if your opponent has opened his guard and forced you to play the open guard, is he who has the upper hand!

2. Keep in touch always

Play open guard requires that the guard player keeps in touch all the time with the opponent. You should always keep 4 points of contact, both the feet and both the hands. With 4 points of contact are you doing Guard, unless he is who is passing his guard. You understand the difference?

3. Use your very feet

Your feet are your first line of defense. You should always use to control the distance and to relieve the pressure that your opponent is doing.

4. Knees are also useful

Knees are your second line of defense. If your opponent has already crossed the line of your feet, you should use the knees to counteract the pressure.

5. Body's Positioning

Your third line of defense is the correct positioning of your body. This includes not to put the back on the floor and do the hip escapes properly.

6. Replacement

The guy is almost passing, or made his guard pass? Do not think of anything other than the replacement! You must return to a position where you feel comfortable!

Some Rules

1. Avoid talking to roll

Nothing more boring than you're rolling, and suddenly the partner pulls a matter of nothing or asks explanation of a position or question as it does to get out of that situation. When you're rolling is to roll and not to talk. Questions must be taken before or after the roll, not during!

2 Do not teach while your instructor is teaching

Always has in throughout the gym, that guy who while the sensei is teaching to position, is talking with his teammate side, saying what to do, or already explaining how does the defense, or questioning the technical efficiency. Do not be you that guy!

3. Wash your kimono

One of the most important tips for sure is this, wash your kimono! Nobody deserves to train with someone who smells bad, and you shouldn't be with field flowers smell or to use your best perfume. Just do not smell bad!

4 Do not wear jewelry during training

Necklaces, bracelets, earrings, rings, all this must be removed and stowed before entering the Mat. These jewels can hurt your training partner, and can especially hurt you.

5- Keep up off the mat if you are sick

As Jiu Jitsu is a very contact sport, if you are sick or with some type of infection, you need to keep away from the mats, so that does not end up passing on the problem to his teammate's training.

6 Sneakers or Shoes in the Mat

A mat is a sacred place, there you learn to give their best and provides your body to a partner train. In this sacred place, there are rules and one of them is that you can only get in, being barefoot. Stepping on the mat using shoes or sneakers, is the total ignorance of culture and martial arts rules. Besides, the shoes can bring all kinds of dirt, which can end up contaminating the mat.

7 Long Nails

Long nails can be dangerous. The nails may scratch and also hurt the eyes and that would be unfair. Therefore, if you do not want to happen with you, start by cutting their own nails, and if you notice that some training partner does not have this habit, talk to him or your sensei for this situation is resolved.

8. Do not talk cuss word

Although people who swear they are more sincere and honest, the mat is no place for using this type of vocabulary. It is a respectful place with you and your training partners, use cuss word may offend people around you.

Chapter 6

Mind Aspects Of Jiu-Jitsu

In the previous chapter, we've seen some of the most common Jiu-Jitsu techniques. While what was represented here is far from a full list, it should provide you with a lot of knowledge necessary to take you a long way on your Jiu-Jitsu journey.

However, this martial art is more than just throws, locks, and strikes. In order to understand and properly apply the techniques of Jiu-Jitsu, it is very important to have the right mental approach and understand the core principles of this ancient discipline.

Importance of being humble

One of the main things those looking to learn Jiu-Jitsu need to remember is to always stay humble. In fact, as your knowledge and your skills grow, so should your humility. There are numerous advantages to staying humble, for you as a practitioner, and for everybody else around you.

Those who manage to stay humble always continue to learn and develop. It is often hard for us to admit that we do not know everything or that we know less than we would like to know. But it is this attitude that results in a willingness to always work on oneself and continuously improve. New ideas can come from the strangest and the least expected of places, and we always have to be open for them. This is not just true for Jiu-Jitsu, but for life in general. If you are capable of incorporating this attitude into your training, then you will probably benefit from it in other areas of your life as well. And so will everyone else.

By staying humble, you will also be able to deal with losses much better. Understanding that you are not the best and, what is more, that even the best have to lose sometimes, will help you get very far in your practice. Put your ego aside and you will be much less frustrated and much more motivated to realize your goals and become the best you can be. It is through humility that one realizes real confidence. If you are humble, it does not mean that you are timid or uncertain, but simply open to realities of life.

Gratitude is another virtue related to humility. Humble people are grateful to those who help them learn and make progress. They are also grateful to those who point out their mistakes Once the ego is removed, it becomes clear to us that people emphasizing our mistakes are doing so not to shame us, but to help us grow and become better. In Jiu-Jitsu, like in other martial arts, it is not uncommon for one to become too self-aware and stop being grateful for the gifts they have been given, and that attitude is counterproductive for someone who wants to grow consistently.

If you want to really master Jiu-Jitsu, you must not become arrogant because of your newly acquired skills which allow you to subdue others. Always remember that the primary function of this ancient martial art is self defense. On the other hand, remove your ego and stay humble in defeat as well. Do not allow for it to frustrate you or shake your confidence. The defeat is necessary on your path to the victory.

Stay relaxed at all times

Apart from always being humble, it is also paramount to stay relaxed at all times for serious Jiu-Jitsu practitioners. Of course, from the point of view someone who is just starting, this may seem impossible. How could you relax when you are about to fight. Isn't it all about being fully tense and ready?

This is, indeed, a hard concept to implement in practice. It is easy enough to say "relax", but actually relaxing while under threat of physical harm is something completely different. It takes some time and a lot of work to wrap your head around it, but once you do, your skills will improve significantly.

Once you learn to relax, you will be less likely to panic in dangerous situations, which will help you make better decisions and find better ways to counter your opponents. Better choices will lead to fewer injuries and better creativity under pressure, which can produce some great results.

Outside the combat, you will have the ability to train longer, and this will reflect on your progress. By staying relaxed, you will also be a better partner for the person(s) you are training with. Even if you are looking to do the most work on your own, you will still need someone to practice with.

All this being said, what are the actual techniques you can employ to relax? One of the most important things to keep in mind is to avoid becoming emotional about things. Your emotions will only cloud your judgment and prevent you from seeing things clearly. Always try to use your mind instead of your heart.

Avoid breathing through the mouth and breath through the nose as much as possible. This will help control your heart rate and help you relax even in the worst of situations.

Stay patient and apply the strategies you know. Forcing things will not get you far, and becoming angry can only work against you. Instead, keep your calm and stick to techniques you have mastered. Panicking will not produce any desirable results. Try to create a plan and then put it in motion. Even if you fail, as long as you stay relaxed, you might get another chance. Once you lose your cool, it will all be over.

Again, being relaxed does not mean being weak or fragile. It is simply a state in which you are able to make full use of the skills you possess and come up with the best strategies even in seemingly very unfavorable situations.

Dealing with frustration

Even if you are the most humble person out there, some frustration is inevitable to creep up from time to time. Like many martial arts, the path to proficiency in Jiu-Jitsu is sprinkled with difficulties.

Repeatedly losing to the same opponent or having difficulties to master certain moves can be quite frustrating; even to the point where you may start to consider quitting. At these times, it is of the utmost importance to try and look at things from a different angle and not let the frustration take over.

Instead, you should turn this negative force around and use it to your advantage. Just like you use your attacker's energy to subdue him, you should learn to channel the energy stemming from any negative feelings and tunnel it into motivation to learn and become better.

There is no learning without trying, and there is no trying without failing. Once you have realized and adopted this notion, the frustration will start to wither away. You should not be angry or frustrated if you are not able to do new things perfectly on your first try. Almost nobody does and this is no cause for concern.

The more you try, however, the better you will get. Understand this and stop torturing yourself about things not developing exactly as you have envisioned.

You can actively work to remove the frustration from your training and your life in general. Always remember that while Jiu-Jitsu is a martial art, it is also a way of life, or at least it is for those who really achieve the success.

Try to have fun once again. At the start of your training, Jiu-Jitsu was probably a lot of fun. You were learning all these new things and techniques, and every day you were happy to know that your skills grew at least a little bit. You can revive that feeling, but you need to do so intentionally. There is no reason for your training not to be fun once again if you firmly decide it will be so.

Likewise, you might need to lower your expectations. Perhaps at the onset, you were progressing quickly, and it seemed as if you will know everything there is to know in no time. Later on, more complex moves came into play, you started learning more difficult strategies, and your progress slowed down. You need to realize that your initial expectations were not realistic and lower the bar. Instead of setting the goals that are almost impossible to achieve, try to be happy about every new thing you learn and enjoy the progress as it comes. That way, your frustration will quickly disappear.

In line with this, you should stay positive at all times. The journey ahead of you is a hard one. There is absolutely no need to approach it with a negative mentality, which will only hold us back. Mistakes are a part of the process, setbacks happen. Focus on things that you do right and be content with them. This is not to say that you shouldn't work to rectify your mistakes, but there is no reason to beat yourself about them either.

Finally, try to avoid comparing yourself to the others on the same path. This can be a cause of a lot of unnecessary frustration. Some people will progress faster. Some of them are more talented than you. Their achievements should not put you down or cause jealousy. Instead, let that be your motivation, not your frustration, and help you train more and harder to become better. Eventually, you will reach your destination if you do the work; the fact that some will get there somewhat sooner should be of no concern to you.

Remember, frustration often leads to enlightenment. Learn to embrace it as a part of the journey and use its energy for your personal progress. Accept the fact that the path ahead of you is a difficult one and don't try to force things. Let everything develop naturally and you will be in a much better mental place overall.

Have patience

Although patience has been mentioned as a part of dealing with frustration, its importance cannot be overstated. Staying patient in the combat and during the training is the only way forward.

During the fight, patience means waiting for the right moment to make your move. Do it too soon, and it will not have the desired effect, and it may even get you in a worse position than you were. Even when you are in a really tight spot, stay patient and wait for the optimal time to strike back.

Outside the combat, patience means accepting that your training is a long journey and that things will not change overnight. Patience will help you overcome even those obstacles that may seem insurmountable.

Chapter 7

Best Exercises For Jiu-Jitsu Practitioners

Mind aspects of Jiu-Jitsu are very important and knowing the right techniques to use in combat is essential, but all of this will serve little purpose if your body is not properly prepared.

Getting your body in proper shape is third and vital part of your journey to dominating Jiu-Jitsu. Regular exercise will help you make sure that you are always ready to take on the challenge, be it a sports competition or a misfortunate situation that requires you to defend yourself.

Regular exercise is even more important if you do not have a partner with whom you can train all the time. Sparring will usually keep you in good shape even if you don't do much outside of fighting training. If you do not have an opportunity to do this on a daily basis, however, these are some exercises that will help you stay in shape between your training sessions.

Practicing breakfalls

We have explained that breakfalls are a very important part of Jiu-Jitsu fighting. You need to master these techniques to avoid frequent injuries that would occur otherwise.

The good thing about breakfalls is that you do not need a partner to practice them, and if you are more hardcore, you can even do it without a mat (although I would not recommend this for new trainees).

Do not let a day pass by without practicing breakfalls for at least half an hour. Pick a particular type and train that one type for as long as you can. Try to do it in a quick, uninterrupted succession: fall, get up, fall again, get up, etc. This way, you will develop natural instincts on how to fall when you find yourself in an actual fight, and you will not have to waste any time actively thinking about which breakfall would be the best in the given situation. You want this to become second nature to you.

Increasing your flexibility

In the discipline like Jiu-Jitsu, where throws, locks, and falls make up the main arsenals of both you and your opponent, being as flexible as possible helps a great deal.

Flexibility will make it easier to perform the moves, to move around, and to escape the grips of your attacker, all without injuring yourself. If you are not flexible, no matter how good your theoretical knowledge is, you will have a hard time putting it to good use.

There are numerous stretching exercises out there that will help you increase your flexibility. I will only mention a few here.

Side lunges. In a standing position, set your legs apart. Bend the left knee, slightly leaning to the left, while keeping your back straight. Stay in this position for five seconds, repeat it a few times, and then switch the legs.

Knees to chest. Lie on the back, with your knees bent. Hold your knees with your hands and bring them slowly to the top of your chest. Repeat a few times, for as long as you don't start to feel too tired.

Seat stretch. Sitting on the floor, with your back straight and your legs stretched straight out, place the hands on your ankles. Move the chin towards the knees, as far as you can. Repeat the exercise at least five times.

Cross-over. While standing, cross your legs and keep the feet close together. Lean forward and try to touch your toes. Stay in this position for about five seconds, then move up and repeat for at least five times.

Muscles and cardio

Although the shear strength is not what Jiu-Jitsu is all about, your physical constitution will play a major role, especially when facing bigger, stronger opponents. Even with the best of techniques, it takes some strength to throw or push someone who has a few pounds on you, so working on your muscles is important, especially when it comes to your legs and arms.

You don't need your muscles to be big necessarily, but you need them to be strong, ready for sudden bursts of energy when the situation requires it. These bursts come from the stored carbohydrates or glycogen in your muscles.

To elevate these levels, you need to perform anaerobic exercises, which do not require oxygen. Bursting exercises, like bursting sprints and squat thrusts will help you build up these elements in your muscles and have them ready to release when facing stronger opponents.

Aerobic exercises, on the other hand, will help you improve your cardio. With rising your heart beat, your body will be receiving more oxygen. This will help you endure longer even when you find yourself in a less favorable position, gripped by your attacker or trying to break his lock. Also, you will recover much faster after such activities.

There are several good exercises for the cardio, and the most efficient ones are the long distance running and jumping rope. But even a long walk every day will help increase that heart beat.

Strengthening your grip

Your grip is another very powerful weapon in Jiu-Jitsu. You will use it to grab your opponents, hold them down in different locks and, sometimes, to break free from their grasp. In any case, having a solid, strong grip will significantly help your fighting performance.

Strangely enough, the grip is often forgotten by many new Jiu-Jitsu practitioners since it does not seem all that important. While it is true that a good technique is more important than the brute force, having a strong, powerful hand certainly doesn't hurt. These are some exercises that can help you improve your grip strength.

Picking up heavy things. Often called deadlift, picking up heavy objects can really increase your grip strength. Since this type of exercise also benefits a number of other muscle groups, many lifters simply use lifting straps to take the grip out of the equation and be able to lift bigger weights. If you are looking to really dominate Jiu-Jitsu, don't do this. Allow for your hands and forearms to be stressed by heavy objects and the more you do it, the more powerful your grip will get.

Climbing is another great exercise for this very purpose. As you climb a rock, you will often find yourself in strange, uncomfortable positions, requiring to hold by the fingertips even. This will do wonders for your grip. Similarly, climbing rope is a great exercise for your hands, wrists and forearms.

Pulling exercises are particularly focused on the grip. In order to really improve, experiment with different handles and try out new things to really challenge yourself. In doing so, your grip will become stronger with each passing day.

Crushing is another grip-focused exercise. It is also very convenient, as you can find a hand gripper in almost every sports store and the practice does not require any particular space. It can even be done while relaxing. There is a variety of grippers out there with different levels of resistance, so find the one that really puts you to the test. Once it becomes too easy, move to the next one.

Clawing is also an excellent way to improve your grip strength. You can do this using a dumbbell, grabbing its hex and lifting it from the ground.

Wrenching. People who spend their days working with wrenches usually have a very strong grip. Hence, tailoring your exercises to mimic this experience can be very effective. If you don't have an idea on how to do it yourself, you can try this. Place one end of a dumbbell in a bucket of rice, with other end sticking out. Grip the outside end of the dumbbell and start twisting back and forth. Do this as forcefully as you can and you will achieve pretty much the same effect that you would with wrenching.

Since all these exercises involve flexor muscles in our hands, it is important to maintain the balance by also training the opposite group of the muscles, called *extensors*. They are in charge of movements in opposite direction.

For this purpose, you can use thick rubber bands placed around the tips of your fingers. Once you put on the band, try to spread your fingers as wide as possible and repeat this exercise 20 - 30 times. Once you feel ready for the challenge, you can find rubber bands with bigger resistance to keep up the pace.

Proper diet

Finally, in order for these exercises to have the best effect and for you to feel your best in general, good diet is also critical. Like in any other sport or martial art, types of food you bring in your body will heavily determine your overall physical shape and effectiveness of your efforts.

Your safest bet is going with natural foods and combine them in such a way to ensure your body gets enough of all necessary ingredients. There are different approaches and advice you can find out there, and this is just one suggestion.

For the purposes of this diet, food is divided into six main large groups:

1) vegetables, meats, fats and seafood

2) starches

3) sweet food and fruits and cheeses

4) acidic fruits

5) milk

6) raw bananas

This diet emphasizes having three meals a day, four and a half hours apart from one another. There are no particular restrictions in terms of food selection, but the important thing is not to combine the foods from different groups in a single meal. This helps to prevent any digestive problems and is also good for keeping your weight in check.

Chapter 8

The Tradition Of The Belts In The Martial Arts

The colored belts were never part of the ancient tradition of Chinese martial arts.

There are many stories about the tradition of the belts in the martial arts, however, the most common is that a novice started his training with a common white belt simply aiming to tie and hold his uniform. As he trained for years, the belt has become dirty, which left her with black and this led to great "fame" of the black belt.

Martial Art in Ancient China

In the old days in China, the person who studied martial arts did not have a predetermined time to advance their hierarchical level, it would evolve as their dedication and ability to assimilate techniques taught.

The Martial Art in the West

Here in the West, because of the difference in our culture, most martial arts has fragmented the content and dividing this content into a system that is required according to their degree within the martial art. This system was created because the practitioners were unmotivated, thinking that lost to the other since it was not clear what the time each one within the sport.

In jiu jitsu this knowledge is represented by belts and degrees.

Learn the meaning of the colors of the belts

White Belt

This is the color of detachment.

White reflects all colors. The very color of this belt indicates that its carrier also has the ingenuity and must maintain a clear mind. However, he has potential, all the colors of the other belts and later as fire is in stone, it is up to him, and do it through the hard training.

The search for this degree is the purification and transformation, before the infinite knowledge you have before yourself. This belt tells us that the beginner should seek humility and creative imagination, by cleaning and clarity of thoughts. It is the rainbow color synthesis and more associated with the sacred because it symbolizes peace, purity, perfection and especially the absolute.

She tells us to seek purity, sincerity and truth; repelling negative thoughts, trying to lift them, to find inner balance, security and develop the instinct and memory.

Blue and Purple Belt

Purple is a mixture of blue and red. This is the color used by the priests to reflect holiness and humility.

It generates feelings of self-respect, dignity and self-esteem.

This is a metaphysical color. It is also the color of alchemy, transformations and magic. It is seen as the color of cosmic energy and spiritual inspiration.

The violet color is excellent for cleansing and healing of physical, emotional and mental levels.

Symbolizes: dignity, devotion, compassion, sincerity, spirituality, purification and transformation. When in bad aspect determines manias and fanaticism.

It is the mystery, expressed a sense of individuality, influencing emotions and moods, but also symbolizes dignity, inspiration and justice. Generates voltage, power, sadness, pity, sentimentality.

Having all this in mind, the color of this graduation tells us that we must find new ways and increase our spiritual intuition.

Brown belt

It is the color of solidification. It is patience, discipline, uniformity acquired and the observation of the rules held to here. Represents the practitioner's connection to the patron of the style that was passed to him, represented by their masters.

To create this color, you need to mix red with black and therefore it has some of its attributes. It also represents the self-criticism and dependency on teachers to get here. It means that you are completing the process of maturing, both in technical knowledge and in the mental aspect.

This track, by its color, exudes the impression of something massive dense, compact.

Suggests security and isolation. also represents a pollution that should always be cleaned by the faithful to the principles of the Budo practice.

A person who likes to dress in brown certainly is extremely dedicated and committed to your work, your family and your friends.

The brown color generates organization and constancy, especially in the everyday responsibilities. People who like to use this color are able to go "to the root of things" and deal with complicated issues in a simple and direct way. Are sensible people.

Black belt

It is the combination of all colors. Finally, the body and mind reached the end of one journey and the beginning of another higher.

The black belt, is humility, self-control, maturity, serenity, discipline, responsibility, dignity and knowledge. It is the color of power, induces the feeling of elegance and sobriety. Where what is outside does not enter and what is inside do not go out.

Note that in most Western societies, black is often the color of death, mourning and penance, thus showing the state of mind to the world, who achieved this graduation.

In general, this color is used by people who reject the conventional rules or are governed by other social norms, such as priests or warriors who follow the Budo.

This color also gives us a sense of tradition and responsibility. It is the absence of vibration of "no color" that gives the feeling of protection or removal.

On the other hand, absorbs, transmutes and returns the negative energies transformed into positive.

The meditation that color allows insight, promotes self-analysis and allows a deepening of the individual in his existential process.

It removes obstacles, unwanted addictions and emotions. The excess brings melancholy, depression, sadness, confusion, loss and fear. The black color is related to the water element that is adapted to all shapes and outlines all obstacles and is the maximum Yin symbol.

Graduation System (belts) Brazilian Jiu Jitsu

The aim of creating a proper grading system of Jiu Jitsu was that there was a standardization and facilitating the teaching and practice of Jiu Jitsu and standardize models championships in Brazil and in the world! Thus, the IBJJF has the Graduation General System, which seeks to make it simple to understand the evolution of the practitioner since the white belt (beginning of all) until the red belt (the highest level of Jiu Jitsu graduation).

Why is there a grading system and belt system in jiu jitsu?

The grading system of jujitsu belts represented by the sequence of jiu jitsu belts was established in order to standardize and facilitate the teaching and practice of Brazilian Jiu-Jitsu, as well as standardize the models of competition and will be presented here as the Generalized System of Undergraduate IBJJF.

The Graduate General System seeks to make simple understanding of the evolution process of each practitioner within the sport from white belt to red belt.

Division of Belts by Age Groups

The graduation system is divided into two large groups of age, being 04-15 years and above 16 years.

It is recommended by the IBJJF initiation of practitioner before 04 years of age.

How to calculate the age of the athlete

The age of the athlete is calculated based on the formula: Current year - Year of birth = Athlete age

Graduation 4 to15 years old

Now separated in groups of colors (gray, yellow, orange and green), the new system for children and young people makes the practice of Jiu-Jitsu much more stimulating and attractive, with more frequent graduations, which provides the steady advance in the activity .

Minimum Ages

White - any age

Gray group (gray and white belt, gray belt, gray and black belt) - 4 to 15 years old

Yellow group (yellow and white belt, yellow belt, yellow and black belt) - 7 to 15 years old

Orange group (orange and white belt, orange belt, orange and black belt) - 10 to 15 years old

Green group (green and white belt, green belt, green and black belt) - 13 and 15 years old

Recommended time for graduation belts

The IBJJF presented as suggestions for teachers and instructors three forms of graduation. There are three different ways to grant degrees to students to mark the time the practice of Jiu-Jitsu within each range of color they are: monthly, quarterly and four months.

Graduation from the 16 years old

Minimum ages for practitioners from 16 years old

White belt - any age

Blue belt - 16 years old or more

Purple belt - 16 years old or more

Brown belt - 18 years old or more

Black belt - 19 years old or more

Red and black belt - 50 years old or more

Red and white belt - 57 years old or more

Red belt - 67 years old or more

Since there is this division of ages, the year in which the athlete complete 16 he should be promoted to the new degree according to the belt you have.

White belt - Stay in white belt

Gray, yellow, orange belt - turns blue belt

Green belt - becomes blue or purple belt according to the decision of the instructor.

In practice, the grading system of the gyms can be done differently recommended by IBJJF.

Minimum Periods in Each Belt

Graduation practitioners also meets the following minimum periods of stay in each color of belt:

Practitioners from 04 to 15 years old - there is no minimum period of stay in each belt.

Practitioners of 16 and 17 years old

White belt - there is no minimum time

Blue belt - there is no minimum time

Purple belt - two years

Practitioners from 18 years old of white belt to brown belt

White belt - there is no minimum time

Blue belt - two years

Purple belt - one year and a half

Brown belt - one year

Practitioners from the black belt

Black belt - 31 years

Red and black belt - 7 years

Red and white belt - 10 years

Red belt - indefinite

The periods for the black belt are fixed and not minimum and determine the time each practitioner should remain in each belt.

Time of the White and Black Belt

The time that the athlete will take to be graduated from white belt to black belt is at the discretion of each teacher and should be obligatorily respected the minimum period of stay in each color of belt.

Black Tip and Degree System

All belts on the jiu-jitsu with the exception of black belt must have at one end a black cloth of 10cm, with spacing of 2.5 to 3 cm of the end of the belt.

The black tip, as is known this tissue serves for the athlete to receive their degrees, which are intermediate graduations between the changes of color of belts.

For practitioners up to 15 years old, IBJJF recommends the system of monthly graduation, quarterly and four months, as already said before, already in over 16 years, are used different recommendations as discussed below.

White, Blue, Purple, Brown - are divided into clear belt plus four degrees.

Black - It is divided into clear belt plus six degrees.

Red and Black - represents the seventh-degree black belt

Red and White - represents the eighth-degree black belt

Red - represents the ninth and tenth-degree black belt

Note: Until the brown belt, the adoption of the degree system is at the discretion of each instructor.

The black belt on is compulsory to adopt degrees defined by IBJJF system.

The black belt is divided into clear belt plus 6 degrees;

The red and black belt is the 7th-degree black belt.

The red and white belt is the 8th-degree black belt.

The eed belt is the 9th and the 10th-degree black belt.

Notes

• The registration form of a senior athlete in white, gray, yellow, orange, green, blue, purple and brown belts must be signed by a black belt in IBJJF registered.

• The graduation of a practitioner to the black belt can only be signed by a professor black belt at least high school graduate by IBJJF.

• The brown belt instructors can only graduate practitioners to purple belt and purple belt instructors can only graduate athletes to blue belt.

How long I get a black belt?

The time that the athlete will take to be graduated from white belt to black belt is at the discretion of each instructor and should be obligatorily respected the minimum period of stay in each belt of color.

What does black belt with a white tip?

A lot of people ask why to use the white tip on the black belt, this is not very common. The white tip is aimed at competing athletes, but its use is optional and can fight the athlete with a black belt or the red end (with or without degrees).

How long from black to coral?

After receiving the black belt, the athlete will be able to reach black belt (red and black) after 31 years of registered black belt.

How old were you can catch the red belt?

The minimum age to conquer the red band is 67 years.

Must you have a test of belt to up to belt?

The test belt is very particular examination of each gym, IBJJF does not impose any technical evaluation as a deterrent for athlete graduation.

What is the green and yellow belt?

You may have noticed that does not appear in the list of graduation green and yellow belts, the reason is that the green and yellow belts are not a graduation belt.

Chapter 9

White and Blue Belts

How to Become White Belt

The Rolls

One of the most basic principles of jiu Jitsu is just learning to minimize the damage caused by falls for it was developed an impact-absorbing system through the rolls.

Description The Rolls

First roll -With your back on the floor and knees out forming a 90 degree angle with the legs is positioned laterally and place your foot on the floor with one of its legs and with the other put it on the leaning side of the ground one of her hands crossed on his chest and hit the other on the floor absorbing the impact, do it on both sides by reversing the position of the feet and hands each time you change the side of the beat.

Second roll - Starting with one knee on the ground and a high base, put the arm on the side of the base that is raised forward and then throw your hand in the space created within the high base, make a turn as a cartwheel rolling over his shoulder and fall in the final position of the first forward roll, with hands on the floor pushing your body back. Attention: throw your knees on the opposite side of the head thus facilitate turning back returning to starting position.

The third roll - Starting up, open the base and make a turn back similar to that taught in the second rolling, back the starting position. Remember at the time of knee turning head to one side to the other.

Fourth Roll - foot base Starting to make a similar move to kick a ball or a slip and let your body touch the ground absorbing the impact with his hand hitting the ground, rest the chin on the chest.

Falls

It is known that in jiu jitsu every fight starts standing so it is very important that you learn techniques that allow design your opponent or at least leave you safer to start your strategy, besides giving you two pontos. Go here a hint: avoid crossing legs to walk on the mat.

Description of Falls

Osoto Gari - Standing, make the grip in kimono his opponent, a hand on the lapel on his chest and the other on the sleeve at the elbow, keep your posture and then a step out to the side of grib made in the elbow, putting her food next to the foot of his opponent and make him support the weight only on one leg that you will beat. Then throw the body forward while you apply the foot passes performing Osoto Gari.

Ogoshi - Make the grip in kimono of his opponent with one of his hands hold the lapel and the other at the elbow, with the hand that was holding the lapel, grab the belt on the back of your opponent then a step crossing toward at the foot of his opponent and with the other leg a step back so that it is inside the base of your opponent and hold the grip, make a turn looking to the side to increase the power of projection.

Ippon Seoinage - Based on the same principle of striking, standing to make the grip in the kimono of your opponent with the lapel and another elbow, keep the grip of elbow high to open space for the hand that was on his lapel, goes below the armpit. Now give a step crossing towards the foot of his opponent and with the other leg a step back so that it is inside the base of your opponent and hold the grip make a turn looking to the side and fit the hip in the space formerly occupied by the hip opponent to increase the power of projection.

Goshi - Make the grip in the kimono of your opponent, with one of his hands hold the lapel and the other behind the neck with the thumb inside, now a step crossing towards the foot of his opponent and with the other leg of a step back so that it is inside the base of your opponent and hold the grip making a turn looking to the side to increase the power of projection.

Tomoenage - Start from striking, grab the kimono of your opponent with one hand on his lapel and another in the elbow, now a step forward and put your foot right next to of your opponent (this time without crossing) while the other leg enters semi-flexed hip his opponent causing a strong lever to roll over your opponent, now sit down very close to him propel him back detail accompanies turning it and fall mounted.

Uchimata - Standing, make the grip in the kimono of your opponent one on the lapel and the other at chest level to keep your lift posture open his footsteps, bringing the elbow your opponent, then a step crossing towards the foot of his opponent and with the other leg a step back, putting in the base of your opponent supporting leg, now with the other leg hit the opponent's leg, looking at the opposite side. Use the hips to get his balance.

Double Leg - To apply the Double Leg, keeps one foot forward (watch out for your opponent does not make any entry in your leg). Make your opponent walks on the mat it will facilitate their entry of fall. Warning: find the proper distance, now, get down to the base touching the front of the knee on the floor, and make the entrance to your shoulder touch the abdomen of his opponent in a fast and explosive movement. The leg that was the basis behind, put laterally beside your body so you will have the basis to take the leg of your opponent from the floor and without strength. Keep the dominant leg and lift up forcing him to support the whole weight on one leg that is on the floor, throw the weight of his opponent for side of the leg supported on the floor and throw successfully completing the Double leg.

Openings and Guard Pass

Once the fight goes to the ground, the great majority of the time the fight falls into the closed guard is a difficult game and little chance for it to arm itself with good openings and guard passes.

Description of the Openings and Guard Passes

Opening guard with knee in the tailbone and pass a hand on the collar - Make grip in the trousers of his opponent, brace your elbows on the inside of the leg of his opponent, supports his knee on his tailbone and push his hip down at the same time pressure with your elbows on the inside of the leg forcing his opponent to open the guard. Hold one of his hands on her hip and the another pummel beneath his opponent's leg leading directly out to the lapel with the big toe, so into putting elbow on the floor and the other hand on his pants, make the grip in the trouser his opponent in that position, or he beats or he gives the pass. He giving, hug the head and control in the 100kg.

Opening Guard standing with Guard Pass - Starting from the closed guard of his opponent to grip in his kimono, holding both lapels for greater control, hold it with your back on the floor and the another grip, hold one of its arms. Now your goal is to stand, for this raise first in the base on the same side of the grip made up his sleeve for him not to hold his leg raised, your second base and pull up as if you were sitting in your lap, keep the grip of the lapel, and with the grip before made up his sleeve, make the grip in the trousers in the high of the knee and force down, forcing his opponent to open the guard. With him already on the ground, kneel on top his knee without that he can close the guard, for this, keep your fingers the foot and the knee on the floor on top the joint of knee him, grab the head decreasing the space between his chest and his opening range and then stabilize.

Submissions

This is the main objective of jiu jitsu since with the withdrawal of his opponent finish the fight, so always look for the finish.

Description of submissions

Americana from Mount - In mount, make the direct grip on the wrist of his opponent, putting him on the ground. Now cross the grip and put your elbow into his ear and pass your other hand under his elbow making key lever called an American. Articulates his arm taking down to pull your leg, now finalize.

Kimura from of 100kg - Starting from 100kg, with one of your hands, hold the head and the other pass below armpit of your opponent making the seat belt grip below the shoulder. With the hand that was holding the head, passes over the face your opponent making the grip on the wrist and throw on the floor with the arm of his opponent at an angle of 90 degrees.

Enjoy your arm that was already beneath his elbow and make the grip in his wrist, stick his elbow along of the body yourself by increasing the amplitude of lever. Now, finalize your opponent.

Kimura from the guard - with his opponent inside your closed guard, force him to support their hands on the floor, choose one of your arms and make the grip directly on the wrist, not in the kimono. Give a spin with your thumb inside (as if speeding a motorcycle) that will make your opponent expose more elbow, get off the hip to the opposite side of the grip on the wrist and move the arm on his arm, but remember: above the elbow with grips made and ready lever, push the arm up, always close to the body and for your opponent don't do the posture, pass your leg over his back.

Arm lock on Mount - mounted on his opponent, dominate one of his arms making the grip behind the elbow, always lift its base to the opposite side of the grip on the elbow. Now fit your opponent in the space created between his leg, stay positioned laterally and pass the leg over the head ending at arm lock.

Arm lock of the closed guard - With his opponent in his closed guard, force it to support your arms on the floor, make the grip in one of the arms with a footprint on the elbow and the other pass underneath and throw the arm to the other side, the hand that is making grip on the biceps hold securely, and the other hand, make the crossed grip on the lapel and pull your opponent, breaking the posture that hampers the defense of the blow.

Now place your foot on the hip on the same side arm dominated, fleeing the hip and up the leg that is free, putting behind the opponent's back helping to keep control, do not release the grips, pass the other leg on the opponent's head and set the arm lock.

Shoulder Blade from guard - Starting spider guard, making its grips direct in the sleeve and then hold one of the grips of the preferred side and with the other hold behind the elbow and pull stretching the leg, straighten and insert the shoulder blade lifting the hips to increase power the coup.

Chokes in jiu jitsu

Choke from the mount - From the mount, enter with the first hand with four fingers inside and enter with the second-hand your thumb inside, move your elbows as if they were touching the ground.

Choke of the guard - use the same techniques described in the previous position, enter the first hand with four fingers inside, enter the second hand of a thumb inside pulling of your opponent, opening elbows and thus finishing.

Rear Naked Choke - it happens when you get the opponent's back with one of his arms wrap the neck of his opponent, making the grip on your other arm in the biceps height, hold firm and with the other hand put behind the opponent's head pushing forward.

Choke of lapel from the back - turns out when you arrive on the back of the opponent, make the grips on the lapel with the thumb inside, involving the neck of his opponent and with the other hand hold the other lapel also with the thumb in and make the choke pulling a lapel to one direction and the other in the opposite direction.

Triangulo of the guard - from spider guard, control the grips on the sleeve of your opponent and climb your legs until you can put your feet on the biceps, keep control. Now, escape the hips and adjust the blow.

Knee On The Belly

Description

Starting from 100kg, grab the head of his opponent, with the other hand that is dominating the hip, loosen the lapel and give to the hand that's holding the head hold fair well, control the leg that is defending the mount and climb the knee that was dominating the hip of your opponent toward the abdomen, firm the base on the ground and do the posture pulling the footsteps giving a pressure on the opponent.

Mount

Starting from 100kg, grab the head of his opponent, with the other hand that is dominating the hip loosen the lapel and to the hand that's holding the head hold fair enough, dominate the leg that will defend the mount, open the range back. Attention: do not relieve the shoulder's pressure on the chin of the opponent, he can just look at one side. Now with your opponent dominated, throw back leg to the range on his body in one swift motion thus winning the mount. Keep your knees on the ground for at least three seconds to worth the scores, hold the grip lapel, pummels his other hand and throw the opponent's arm, crossing over your neck take the hand grip made in his lapel and end the RNC, but with the arm inside, use hand on the forehead do the position until your opponent give up the fight giving the tap out.

Blue Belt

Defense. This is the word, you will not be a good blue belt unless you have a decent defense.

A good blue belt should be able to escape the main positions with relative ease, it's a degree that the game is built on top of the defense.

Movements in sequence

It is when also begins to make movements in sequence, such as a defense arm lock against attacking with a guard passing attack, a sweep followed by the mount, finishing with a sweep, so will building a solid game and have another of jiu jitsu vision. We see a more competitive jiu jitsu and getting harder after all the black belt, which is the professional level, approaches every step.

What is expected of a blue band (goals)

1. 5 choke blows and keys on guard.

2. 2 choke blows and key in half guard

3. 5 choke blows and keys 100 kg

4. 3 detentions

5. 3 choke blows to the mount (front)

6. 3 escape from mount (front)

7. 5 choke options and a lock in the back grip.

8. 2 back grip escapes.

9. 4 guard passes

10. Scores

11. 4 blows options All Fours

12. 5 falls

13. 5 fights

14. History of Jiu Jitsu.

And of course, what is expected of a blue belt as well as all other belts are ethical values, discipline, respect, honor, dedication and etc ...

If you have to point out the three most common mistakes of the blue belts.

1. The first is sure to be the posture. They are caught several times in the triangle or are swept off to be with the wrong posture.

2. The second is that the blue belts, lose the posture for attempting to put the two hooks at once. The fix that is to pull the opponent over them and put a hook at a time.

3. The third mistake is the use of force during combat. The inexperience, they tend to prefer the use of force on the technique, forgetting that the jiu jitsu is the gentle art.

Importance of the Rolls in Jiu Jitsu

The rolls are basically techniques of falls, whose main function is to protect the parts of your body in various situations of falls, softening the impact with the ground, preventing injuries, and giving you agility movements.

Basic rolls

One of the first things we learn when we started in Jiu Jitsu is the roll series (ukemi). The rolls are very important parts to our Jiu Jitsu evolve.

Rolls in other Martial Arts

As mentioned, the rolls are designed to protect from falls, therefore, they are also used in other martial arts such as Aikido and Judo, being Judo the art with more variations of this plea.

General Tips for Jiu Jitsu athletes

1- Practice Jiu Jitsu whenever you can

Whenever you can, make by yourself repetitions of movements like escape of the hip (pushing air with arms). Strengthen the neck movements and stretches.

2- Have a partner to train Jiu Jitsu

Get a partner to do with you many repetitions of basic movements. For example, the closed guard, lift the body and attach to Kimura on both sides. Then lift up to open the friend's closed guard.

3- Workout off the mat

The white belt usually does a lot of strength. Exercising the muscles off the mat, to strengthen the body and ligaments and avoid lesões.

4- Do not miss the training

Start by going to two classes per week. With time, go to three. Go increasing your workload gradually. But do not miss, not by muscle pain. Lengthen well is vital to reduce the pain.

5. Prevent

In breaks of the training, do not let your legs straight on the way. There are other training and you can hurt.

6- Always keep the fighter posture

Keep always together elbows from your body. Create the habit in all positions even walking down the street.

7. Learn to pull to the Guard

In the beginning, learn to pull to the closed guard. Even players like the UFC's champions already seriously injured the knee by not keeping proper posture when a colleague pulled into the closed guard. Safety is everything.

8 Defense, Defense, Defense

Practice the escapes of the submissions at the time of repetition, not in sparring training. Beat when the blow is fitted before force any joint.

9. Your body will give signs

To feel a little pain, tell your instructor. He can spend a few exercises to repeat to stop the pain. In the long run, you will end up training a lot more because of it.

10- Train the technique

At first, make the repetitions slowly. Working the technique does not speed.

Chapter 10

Learn Jiu Jitsu More Easily

The four stages of learning

In the globalized world we can say with some certainty that we are in the Information Age, new information coming in all the time and whenever we come across new information we have two possibilities:

1. Distort it and look fit into our old categories.

2. Leave the new information to organize by itself.

Learning is a skill that is divided into four stages:

Unconscious incompetence

We do not know to do something, and we do not know we do not know. If someone has never driven a car, he has no idea what that means.

Let's say a rookie fighter. He has absolutely no idea how to position your hands, arms, head and body when he is in the custody of the opponent. As a result, it is being bombarded with arm locks, finishing attacks and sweeps all the time.

The solution is of course to the fighter on guard to maintain good posture, but in the first phase he never even heard of the concept of posture.

He has no idea that posture would make your life much easier, allowing avoid the guard and start working the guard pass. He is both incompetent in not maintain posture, and unconscienced that is even something he should be doing.

Conscious incompetence

You recognize that there is something you should be better, but you still have difficulty implementing it.

Then one begins to learn to drive and soon discover its limitations. Learn consciously shift gears, step on the clutch, brake, etc. And all his attention back to it, but the person is not competent and drives only on less busy streets.

You are training a month or two, and is finally starting to realize that there is a reason for your coach is always yelling "posture, posture, posture!"

Now, you recognize that posture is important, but not yet understand what exactly is the position and how to practice it. He knows that should do "things" to maintain good posture, but this thing is he does not know exactly for sure.

Conscious competence

You know how to do something, but it is not instinctive. You still need to focus on the ability, in order to do it properly.

We can drive, but need a lot of concentration. We learn technique, but we still need a lot of concentration to put into practice.

Now you have trained frequently and is getting much better do the posture to the guard.

If someone tries to pull it to the guard, then you know all kinds of tricks to prevent this from happening, including good grips, posture and keep your back opponent on the floor.

More still have to think about it, but you finally became competent in doing the posture. This is a big step, but it is not the ultimate goal.

Unconscious competence

At this stage the skill in question has become "second nature" and you no longer have to think about it.

And this is our goal. All small patterns that we learn with much effort, come together in a harmonious unit of behavior. And from then on, we can admire the scenery, listen to the radio and talk while driving. Our conscious mind sets the goal and lets the unconscious take care of it, releasing attention to other things.

After a thorough training, we managed to reach the fourth stage and form habits. At this point, the ability became unconscious. However, habits are not always the most efficient way to perform a task. Our beliefs and knowledge accumulated in the course of our lives end up filtering and making us lose some information that is essential to get to unconscious competence.

All are important

Of course, the four stages of learning apply all the skills you learn, not just doing posture on the guard! Applies to learn the level of change, applies to defend the neck when the opponent is mounted, applies to ride a bike, drive a car, or cook a perfect omelette. The four stages of learning is a very useful model!

Simply identify a deficiency in your arsenal, or become aware that the problem still exists, it has moved from one phase to phase two in the four stages of learning. What you need to do is learn the technical details, make thousands of repetitions to "root" it in your mind, and spend tons of time using this technique with training partners and you will be at level four.

Chapter 11

Final Advice To Dominate Jiu-Jitsu

By this point, you should have everything you need to really start dominating Jiu-Jitsu, from the core philosophy to techniques used, necessary mindset and exercises to keep you in shape at all times and help you develop. So, what else is needed?

To be able to implement the techniques listed here, you will need to practice, and practice a lot. Jiu-Jitsu is very demanding and not very forgiving. If you are not ready to work on developing your skills, you will not get very far. Constant training is the only certain way to success.

Likewise, you will need exercise regularly, or you will get injured often, and this can turn you away from the training. Make enough time in your day for exercises to slowly bring your body in shape for the challenges ahead. Preparation is the key to success in many activities, and this is particularly the case in Jiu-Jitsu.

Regular exercise following the advice mentioned here will help you move forward.

While mastering techniques and physical exercises is difficult, getting in the right mind frame for success is probably the hardest thing for most people. Staying humble, focused and grateful often does not come naturally, it is something that needs to be learned.

The learning process is hard and not without its obstacles, but you must not become discouraged. Accept everything that comes your way as a part of the journey, embrace your mistakes and learn from them, and enjoy your successes. Stay positive about every little step forward you make and try not to compare yourself to others. Your success is your own, and it is not connected to anyone else. If anything, let successes of others serve as motivation on your path to dominating Jiu-Jitsu.

Most importantly, enjoy it. If you approach the Jiu-Jitsu training as something that you have to do, you are not likely to succeed. The challenges might prove to be too difficult. On the other hand, if you accept it as something you want to do and look forward to doing, you will set yourself up for success.

Enjoy the training, be happy about the fights, win or lose, and accept the daily exercise as something that benefits you overall. Jiu-Jitsu is not just a martial art, it is a way of life for real practitioners, and that is what you are aiming to become. By finding joy in your efforts, they will seem much less like efforts and much more like real achievements.

The power of repetition in Jiu Jitsu

Practice makes perfect, especially when dealing with an art that is growing every day with techniques invented every minute. All this is due to a generation of athletes who went to study and practice jiu jitsu, a generation that is revolutionizing this exciting gentle art called jiu jitsu.

Repetition

Act or effect to repeat.

In the teachings of Lord Miyagi, Daniel San in the classic movie "The Karate Kid", the master uses as one of its teaching methods the repetition.

To arrive at its best, the main character of the film repeats movements in day to day activities. Repetition is key to improving techniques and let the movements and reflexes "automatic".

The power of repetition in jiu jitsu

It is a classic in the jiu jitsu hear the Master the following sentence: "If you want to learn to have to repeat" or "Ten is not enough to make 50".

The learning implies directly the acquisition of new information or knowledge that are retained in memory and motor learning, in turn, results in the acquisition of new skills of procedures.

Therefore, it is required a minimum of practice of motor skills to occur improvements observable in performance.

It is through the repetition of a motor skill that retaining this ability occurs, so that there is a conversion of the original features of unstable memory (short term memory) in a stable form (long term memory), robust and resistant to degradation over a period of time.

So to repeat thoroughly positions and blows, do not only over a day but also during a period when we train this position (eg before a championship), we do not longer forget the positions and apply them on instinct, it seems that body responds to the stimulus alone. Another way of learning is watching the training. When watching repetitively the positions, we just recording and taking that knowledge to a deeper level, to what we call stable. Who never applied a blow or made a posture and said, gee how I did it? That's because you in any time coached or watched and learned this position or blow and was retained in his knowledge of stable memories (long term memory).

Drill

Today in the modern jiu jitsu is much talk in functional training, specific training, but notes the notoriety that has been given to the drill, which is a series of exercises designed to improve and enhance certain skills which have difficulty performed them. It is how to divide the training into parts to improve only where we want to perform better.

Tip

The first form of learning jiu jitsu is looking, so instructors always warn of the importance of looking at the senior training, through the eyes we come to "grasp the game" that Thick-skinned of the gym thanks to the mirror neuron.

We, humans, have an innate facility to imitate gestures, words and actions of others, a feature that is both useful to know how to recognize, that is, the mirror neurons of an individual both mimic and reflect (and feel) the actions of others.

And so, in this way, the viewer realizes and feels the same of what we observe, and hence the name of mirror neurons. This may prove to empirically when we see that small children smile when we smile in front of you.

Interestingly, something very similar to this phenomenon exists in traditional Japanese culture, where an expression describes this fact:

Learn looking closely and mimicking the gestures of those who teach.

Conclusion

Thank you again for downloading this book!

After reading these pages, you should know everything you need to know about Jiu-Jitsu. You now know how this martial art came to be, what was it original purpose, and how it changed over time.

Some basic techniques and exercises have been presented for your benefit as well. If you really apply yourself to learning what was described in this book, you should quickly advance on your quest to dominating Jiu-Jitsu.

The rest is up to you and how much you want to succeed. Knowledge alone is not enough without proper implementation, so you will need to work hard to develop your skills and learn something new every day to keep you interested and motivated.

Once you feel you have advanced enough on your own, it may be time to look for a Jiu-Jitsu school nearby and take your training to the next level. Benefits of getting into such a program are numerous, as you will have a trainer to guide you along as well as access to other trainees to practice with on regular basis.

The important thing is that you will not be getting into it completely in the dark. If you have learned the techniques from this book and properly applied exercises listed in here, you will be far ahead of other new students and your progress will be very fast, guaranteed!

Finally, if you enjoyed this book, then I'd like to ask you for a favor, would you be kind enough to leave a review for this book on Amazon? It'd be greatly appreciated!

George Silva

George Silva

Made in United States
North Haven, CT
12 June 2023

37643327R00059